MW00581742

CAMBRIDGE
Global English

for Cambridge Primary English as a Second Language

Workbook 1

Elly Schottman, Caroline Linse & Paul Drury

Series Editor: Kathryn Harper

CAMBRIDGE
UNIVERSITY PRESS

University Printing House, Cambridge CB2 8BS, United Kingdom

One Liberty Plaza, 20th Floor, New York, NY 10006, USA

477 Williamstown Road, Port Melbourne, VIC 3207, Australia

314–321, 3rd Floor, Plot 3, Splendor Forum, Jasola District Centre, New Delhi – 110025, India

79 Anson Road, #06–04/06, Singapore 079906

Cambridge University Press is part of the University of Cambridge.

It furthers the University's mission by disseminating knowledge in the pursuit of education, learning and research at the highest international levels of excellence.

www.cambridge.org
Information on this title: www.cambridge.org/9781108963640

© Cambridge University Press 2021

First published 2014
Second edition 2021

20 19 18 17 16 15 14 13 12 11 10 9 8 7 6 5 4 3 2 1

Printed in Dubai by Oriental Press

A catalogue record for this publication is available from the British Library

ISBN 978-1-108-96364-0 Workbook with Digital Access (1 Year)

Additional resources for this publication at www.cambridge.org/9781108963640

....

Contents

How to use this book

This workbook provides questions for you to practise what you have learned in class. There is a unit to match each unit in your Learner's Book.

Colour the stars at the beginning of each unit as you learn to do each thing.

Tips to help you with your learning.

Words to help you with your writing.

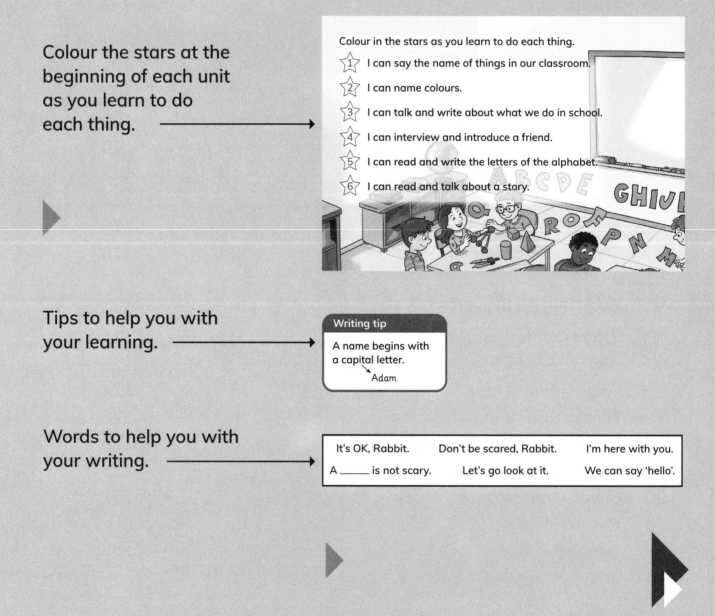

Colour in the stars as you learn to do each thing.

1. I can say the name of things in our classroom.
2. I can name colours.
3. I can talk and write about what we do in school.
4. I can interview and introduce a friend.
5. I can read and write the letters of the alphabet.
6. I can read and talk about a story.

Writing tip

A name begins with a capital letter.

Adam

| It's OK, Rabbit. | Don't be scared, Rabbit. | I'm here with you. |
| A _____ is not scary. | Let's go look at it. | We can say 'hello'. |

Each Use of English lesson is divided into three different levels. You can choose the level that is right for you.

Focus: these grammar questions help you to master the basics.

Practice: these grammar questions help you to become more confident in using what you have learned.

Challenge: these questions will make you think very hard.

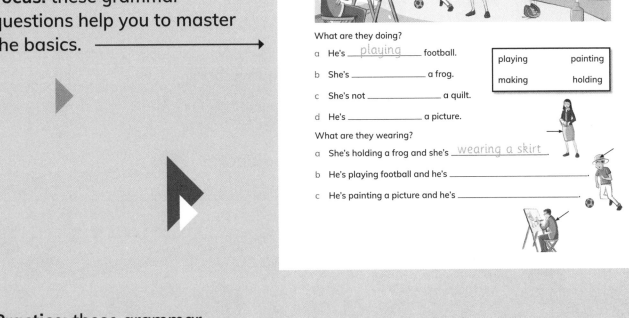

Focus

1 **Look at the pictures.**
   Complete the sentences using words from the box.

What are they doing?

a He's ___playing___ football.

b She's _____ a frog.

c She's not _____ a quilt.

d He's _____ a picture.

| playing | painting |
| making | holding |

What are they wearing?

a She's holding a frog and she's ___wearing a skirt___

b He's playing football and he's _____

c He's painting a picture and he's _____.

Practice

3 **Complete the robot picture.**
   Read the sentences to finish drawing the robot.
   a The robot is on a table.
   b The robot is under an umbrella.
   c The left leg is next to the right leg.
   d The robot has a hat on his head.
   Now write two more sentences and add to your picture.
   e The cat is _____ the robot.

   f _____

Challenge

Find something in your classroom that is made of **metal** or **plastic**. Draw a picture.

This is made of _____.

1 ▶ Welcome to school

Colour in the stars as you learn to do each thing.

☆1 I can say the name of things in our classroom.

☆2 I can name colours.

☆3 I can talk and write about what we do in school.

☆4 I can interview and introduce a friend.

☆5 I can read and write the letters of the alphabet.

☆6 I can read and talk about a story.

> 1.1 What do we do at school?

1 Count and write.

Write the numbers. Add an **-s** at the end of the words to show more than one.

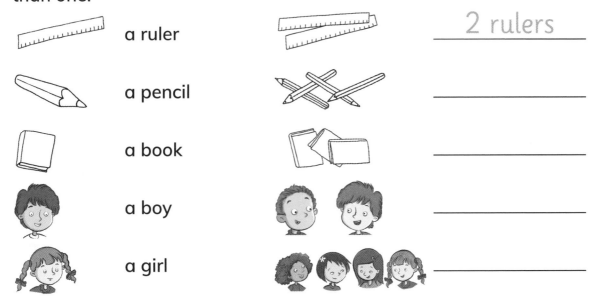

a ruler _____2 rulers_____

a pencil _____

a book _____

a boy _____

a girl _____

2 Draw your face and colour your lunchbox.

Trace the words in the speech bubbles.

Hi!
What's your name?

My name is
_____

I like your
lunchbox.

Thank you!

› 1.2 In the classroom

1 What's in your classroom? Trace the words and (circle) yes or no.

Classroom treasure hunt			
an orange chair Colour the chair.		yes	no
a green pencil Colour the pencil.		yes	no
a red book Colour the book.		yes	no
a brown table Colour the table.		yes	no
a black crayon Colour the crayon.		yes	no
a clock		yes	no
a computer		yes	no

2 Write your own *Hello school!* poem.

Choose words from the box.

Draw a picture. Read your poem to a partner.

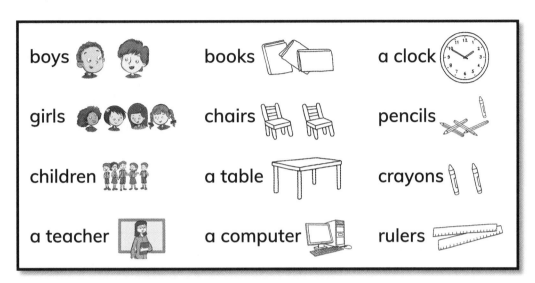

boys	books	a clock
girls	chairs	pencils
children	a table	crayons
a teacher	a computer	rulers

_____ and _____,

A list of rules

_____ and _____,

Hello, school!

〉 1.3 Children around the world

1 Write and draw.

Write 3 sentences about you. Draw a picture of you.

Choose words from the box.

What's your name?

My name is _____.

How old are you?

I am _____.

What do you do at school?

_____ at school.

Writing tip

A name begins with a capital letter.

Adam

read

write

draw

sing

do maths

use computers

2 Fill in the chart.

Look at the chart. Answer the questions.

How do you go to school?						
I go by bus.	Lara	Aron	Tanya	Ali	Paco	
I go by car.	Kuldip	Marta	Sara			
I go by bicycle.	Lucas					
I walk.	Pablo	Dina				

a How many children go by bus? __5__

b How many children go by car? _____

c How many children go by bicycle? _____

d How many children walk? _____

e How do <u>you</u> go to school?
   Write your name on the chart.

Challenge

Talk to your friend.

How does your friend go to school? _____

> 1.4 This is my friend

Focus

1 **Trace and complete the sentences.**
Then colour in the balloons.

My name is Fatima. I am 7. My favourite colour is red.

This is Fatima. She's 7.
Her favourite colour is red.

My name is Anuman. I am 9. My favourite colour is blue.

My name is Marat. I am 8. My favourite colour is green.

This is Anuman.
He's 9. His favourite colour is blue.

This is Marat. He's 8.
His favourite colour is green.

My name is _____. I'm _____.
My favourite colour is _____.

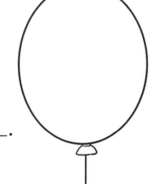

Practice

2 Read and match.

Read the sentences carefully. Then colour and complete the pictures.

Her name is Lara. Her book is green. Colour it in.

She is 7. Colour her age on her badge.

His name is Aron.

His book is blue. Colour it in.

He is 6. Colour his age on his badge.

My name is

_____

My name is

_____

Challenge

3 Write about your friend.

Describe and draw your partner. Use *his* or *her*.

This is my friend.

_____ name is _____.

_____ favourite colour is _____.

_____ is   6   7   8   9.

› 1.5 The alphabet

1 Capital letters

Trace and then write the missing capital letters. Say the rhyme.

A B __ D E __ G

We're in school, you and me.

H __ J __ L __ N

I have a pencil. You have a pen.

O __ Q R __ T

Look around. What do you see?

U V __ X Y __

Put your hands on your head!

2 Trace and match.

Trace the letters. Match the letters to the pictures.

Bb Cc Ff Hh Tt Ll Rr Pp

3 Word wall

| boy | bus | computer | clock | car | book |

Look at the box.
What letter do the words begin with?

Write the words under **Bb** or **Cc** and draw pictures.

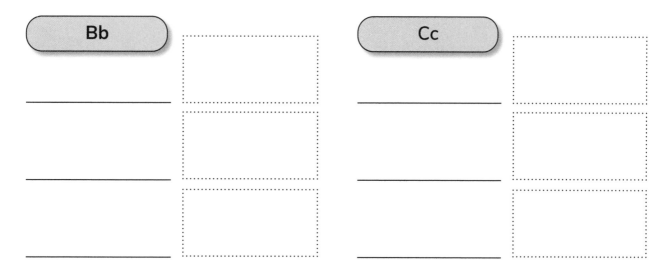

Bb

Cc

_____

_____

_____

_____

_____

_____

Challenge

Add one more word for each letter. Draw a picture.

b _____   c _____

4 Mystery words

Look at the first letter of the missing words.

Draw a line to the picture that begins with that letter.

a I see a t_____.

b I see a p_____.

c I see a c_____.

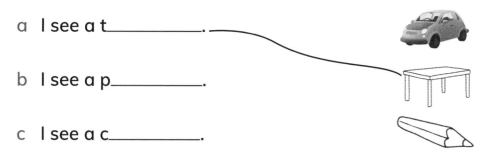

> 1.6 What do you see?

1 **Would you see it in the classroom or outside?**

Draw a line from the small pictures to the big picture.

clock

whiteboard

car

flowers

birds

2 **How do you feel when you see these things?**

Write the word and draw the face.

happy   curious   surprised

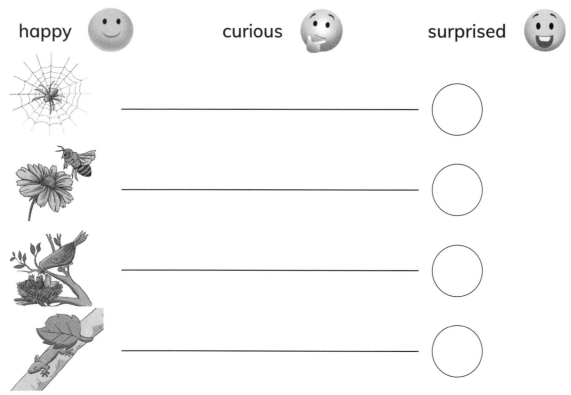

3 **Write and draw.**

What do you see on your way to school, and how do you feel?
Choose words from the box.
Draw a picture.
Read your story to a partner.

On the way to school, I see _____

_____

I feel _____

〉 1.7 Check your progress

Listen to your teacher. Tick (✔) the correct pictures.

1

2

3

Listen and colour.

4
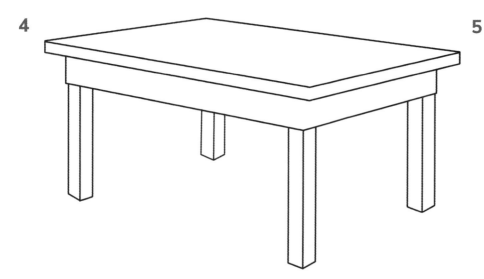

5
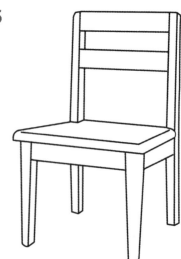

Read and write.

6   Write your name.

My name is _____.

Reflection

Talk with a partner.

What was your favourite activity in this unit?

_____

_____

Which activity was the hardest?

_____

_____

Name 3 new words you learned.

_____

_____

_____

2 Family time

Colour in the stars as you learn to do each thing.

1 ⭐ I can talk about families.

2 ⭐ I can count and write numbers 0–10.

3 ⭐ I can ask and answer questions about food.

4 ⭐ I can read and write words with short **a**.

5 ⭐ I can read and write about what families do.

〉 2.1 What do families do together?

1 Girls and boys

Who is a man or a boy?

Who is a woman or a girl?

Write the words in the correct list.

~~mother~~   ~~father~~

grandma   grandpa   brother

sister   me

	father		mother
	_____		_____
	_____		_____
	_____		_____

2 Look and count.

How many people are in Sam's family?

There are _____

people in Sam's family.

How many people are in your family?

There are _____
people in my family.

❯ 2.2 At home

1 Finish the sentences.

Who do you talk with?

Use the words in the box to complete each sentence.

I talk with

_____.

I play with

_____.

I sing with _____.

I go to school with _____.

my mum	my grandpa
my teacher	my dad
my sister	my friend
my brother	my grandma

2 This is for you!

Write a name on the gift tag. Then draw a gift in the box.

For
_____

3 Make a card.

Write and draw a card for a friend.

a   Make a plan. Talk with a partner or your class.

Who is your card for? _____

What do you and your friend like to do together?

_____

What will you write in your card? Here are some ideas.

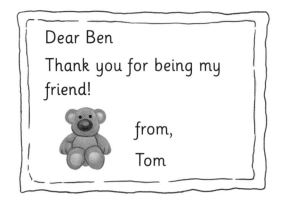

Dear Ben
Thank you for being my friend!
from,
Tom

Dear Maya,
You are my friend.
I like you.

Love,
Serena

b   Write your message.
Write your name at the end.

Dear _____ ,

_____

_____

_____

Dear Daniel
This card is for you!

from,
Stefan

c   Next, make a real card with paper, scissors and crayons.
On the front of the card, draw a picture of you and your friend.
Write a message inside.

› 2.3 Let's count!

| 0 | 1 | 2 | 3 | 4 | 5 | 6 | 7 | 8 | 9 | 10 |

1 How many?

Count the things. Write the numbers.

a There is _____ table.   d There are _____ windows.

b There are _____ chairs.   e There are _____ rabbits.

c There is _____ door.   f There are _____ ducks.

2 Add numbers.

Write the missing numbers.
Say the number sentences.

One add one
equals two.

$1 + 1 = 2$

$3 + 1 =$ _____ $6 + 3 =$ _____

3 **Take away numbers.**

Write the missing numbers. Sing the song!

There are 10 in the bed.

2 fall out. | $10 - 2 =$ _____ |

There are 8 in the bed.

2 fall out. | $8 - 2 =$ _____ |

There are 6 in the bed.

2 fall out. | $6 - 2 =$ _____ |

There are 4 in the bed.

2 fall out. | $4 - 2 =$ _____ |

There are 2 in the bed.

2 fall out. | $2 - 2 =$ _____ |

Good night!

There are 0 in the bed.

And everybody says,
'Good night!'

❯ 2.4 What do you eat for breakfast?

Focus

1 Spin and answer.

Use a pencil and a paper clip. Play with a partner.

Take turns to spin the paper clip. Ask your partner if they like the food.

Practice

2 Which foods do you and your partner like and not like?

😊 I like _____.

🙁 I don't like _____.

😊 My partner likes _____.

🙁 My partner doesn't like _____.

3 What else do you and your partner like?

😊 I _____.

😊 My partner _____.

4 Zara is shopping for her mum.
Read the sentences and write the missing words.

Draw a path through the market.

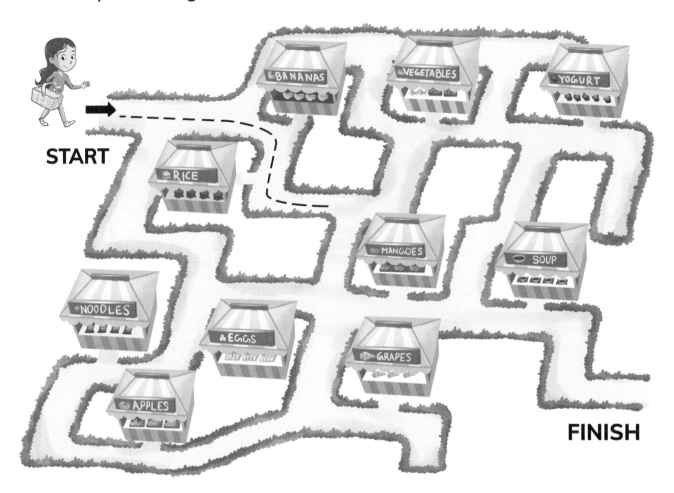

a   Mum likes bananas.   d   <u>She likes</u> apples.

b   She likes rice.   e   _____ likes mangoes.

c   <u>She likes</u> noodles.   f   _____ soup.

Challenge

Use a different colour to draw another path through the market.
Then write the sentences.

› 2.5 Short a

1 Read and draw.

Read the sentences out loud. Complete the pictures.

Dad has a hat.   Mum's cap is black.

A cat is on my lap.

2 Short **a** sound.

Circle and say the words that have the short **a** sound.

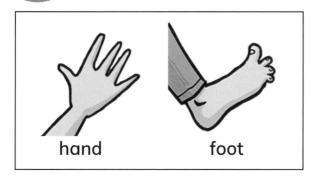

hand   foot

stand   sit

dog   cat

write   clap

dad   mum

apple   egg

3 Write the words.

Look at the words in Activity 2.
Write the words for these pictures in the boxes below.

a

| c | l | a | p |

b
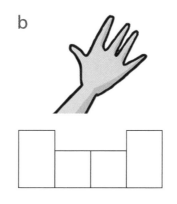

c
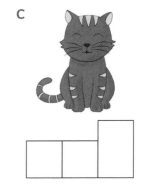

> 2.6 Three families

1 What day is it today?

Circle your answer.

Monday   Tuesday   Wednesday
Thursday   Friday   Saturday   Sunday

Is there a calendar in your home?   yes   no

Is there a calendar in your classroom?   yes   no

2 Whose shopping list?

These families are shopping in three different shops.

Each family has a shopping list.

Draw a line from the shopping list to the matching picture.

ball
car
kite

mangoes
bananas
eggs

bed
chair
table

Food Shop

Toy Shop

For The Home

3 Write and draw.

What do you and your family like to do together?

a   Plan your work. Read the list with a partner. Tick (✔) your answers.
    Write one more answer!

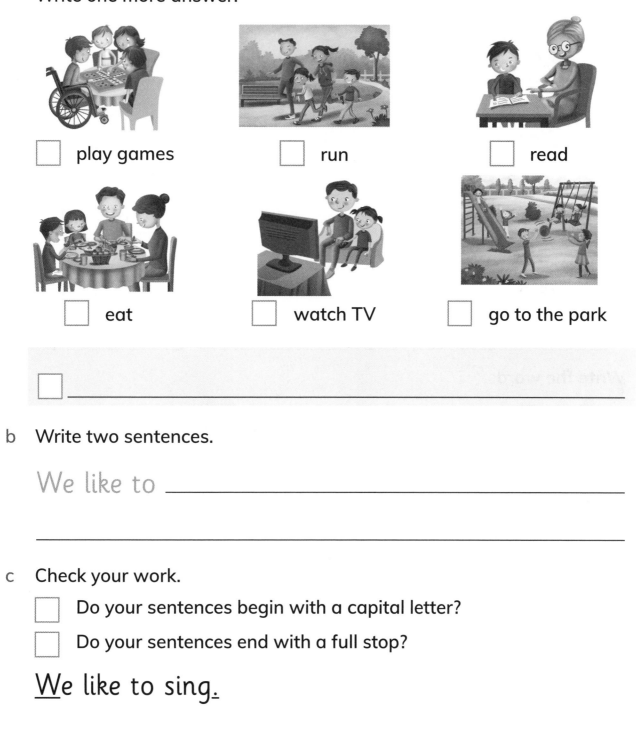

☐ play games   ☐ run   ☐ read

☐ eat   ☐ watch TV   ☐ go to the park

☐ _____

b   Write two sentences.

We like to _____

_____

c   Check your work.

☐ Do your sentences begin with a capital letter?

☐ Do your sentences end with a full stop?

We like to sing.

> 2.7 Check your progress

Listen to your teacher. Tick (✔) the correct pictures.

Write the words.

5 _____ _____ _____   6 _____ _____ _____

Read the sentences. Tick (✔) the correct pictures.

7 Dad has a hat.

a ☐   b ☐

8 I like apples.

a ☐   b ☐

Reflection

Talk with a partner.

What is your favourite thing to do in English class?

☐ sing songs   ☐ draw and write   ☐ play counting games

☐ read stories   ☐ ask and answer questions

We learn to **talk**, **read** and **write** in English class.
What do you want to work on the most?

☐ I want to **talk** in English.   ☐ I want to **read** in English.   ☐ I want to **write** in English.

35 〉

Colour in the stars as you learn to do each thing.

⭐ 1   I can talk about things we can do.

⭐ 2   I can follow instructions and play games.

⭐ 3   I can read and write words with short **u**.

⭐ 4   I can say where things are (*on*, *next to*, *under*).

⭐ 5   I can act out a play and talk about characters.

> 3.1 Let's have fun!

bounce	catch	hit	kick	roll	~~throw~~

1 What can we do with a ball?

Write the missing words from the *box*.

 We can _____throw_____ a ball.

 We can _____ a ball.

 We can _____ a ball.

 We can _____ a ball.

 We can _____ a ball.

 We can _____ a ball.

Challenge

What is your favourite thing to do with a ball?

I like to _____ a ball.

> 3.2 Can you do it?

1 What can you do?

Read the question. Try it! Can you do it?

(Circle) **yes** or **no**. Then write a sentence: Yes, I can. or No, I can't.

a   Can you **bounce** a ball 4 times?   **Yes**   **No**

_____

b   Can you **throw** a ball into a box?      **Yes**   **No**

_____

c   Can you **catch** a ball with a box?      **Yes**   **No**

_____

d   Can you **roll** a ball and **hit** a box?      **Yes**   **No**

_____

2 Draw and write.

Work with a partner.
What can you do with a
 ball and a box?

Try it out! Then draw a
picture and write.

I can _____

_____

_____

3 Trace the numbers.

Write the missing numbers.

1 2 ___ 4 ___ 6

7 ___ 9 10 ___ 12

4 Count and write.

How many children? _____

How many books? _____

Draw a line from each child to a book.
Are there more children or more books?

_____

Challenge

Draw some books so that every child has a book.

How many books will you draw?

_____

〉 3.3 Games from around the world

1 Match the picture.

Read each sentence. Draw a line to the matching picture.

a **Scissors** can cut paper.

b **Paper** can cover a rock.

c A **rock** can break scissors.

2 Compare games.

Look again at the Learner's Book (pages 54 and 55).

Think about the games Rock, paper, scissors and Bird, water, rock.

How are they similar? How are they different?

Write the words in the chart.

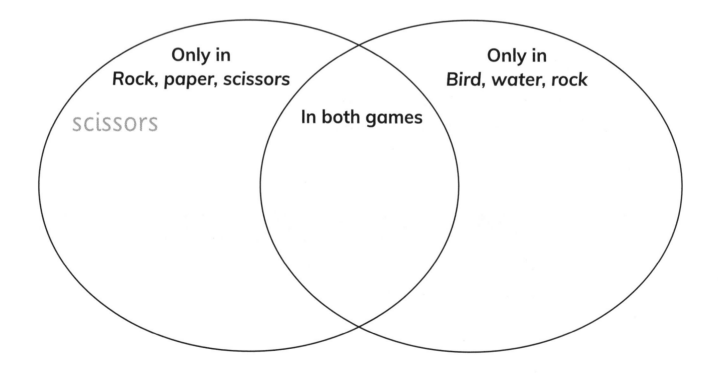

Only in
Rock, paper, scissors

scissors

In both games

Only in
Bird, water, rock

3 Play Rock, paper, scissors.

Play the game five times with a partner and write the name of the winner.

Rock, paper, scissors	
	The winner is …
Game 1	
Game 2	
Game 3	
Game 4	
Game 5	

Be a good sport!

Use these words as you play the game.

You win.

Well played!

Let's play again.

4 Play Bird, water, rock.

Play the game five times with a partner and write the name of the winner.

Bird, water, rock	
	The winner is …
Game 1	
Game 2	
Game 3	
Game 4	
Game 5	

> 3.4 Where is the duck?

Focus

1 Read, colour and draw.

Colour this hat blue.

Colour this hat black.

Colour this ball green.

Draw another hat and colour it your favourite colour.

Colour this ball yellow.

2 Complete the sentences.

Look at the picture. Write words to complete the sentences.

| on | next to | under | above |

a   The black hat is _____ on _____ the duck.

b   The blue hat is _____ the black hat.

c   The green ball is _____ the duck.

d   The cat is _____ the table.

Practice

3 Complete the robot picture.

Read the sentences to finish drawing the robot.

a   The robot is on a table.

b   The robot is under an umbrella.

c   The left leg is next to the right leg.

d   The robot has a hat on his head.

Now write two more sentences and add
to your picture.

e   The cat is _____ the robot.

f   _____

Challenge

4 Complete the sentences.

Look at the picture. Complete the sentences to show where they are.

a   Milly is _____next to_____ Molly.

b   Emily is _____
    Milly and Molly.

c   Hannah is _____on_____
    Milly and Molly.

d   Emily is _____ Elly.

e   Where is Emma? Emma is

    _____.

Milly

Emma

Elly

> 3.5 Short u

1 Sort the words.

Look at the box.

Write the words into the correct lists and then say the words.

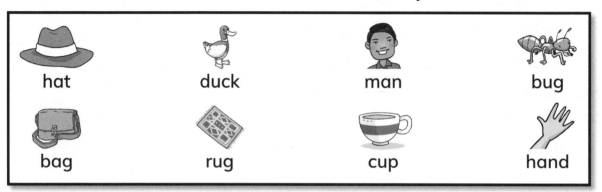

| hat | duck | man | bug |
| bag | rug | cup | hand |

short **u** sound
duck

short **a** sound
bag

2 Write the words.

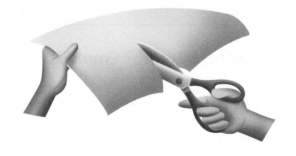

The scissors __ __ __ the paper.

I __ __ __ in the park.

Challenge

Finish the sentence with two words from the box in activity 1. Draw it.

The _____ is on the _____.

3 Crossword puzzle

Look at the pictures. Write the words.

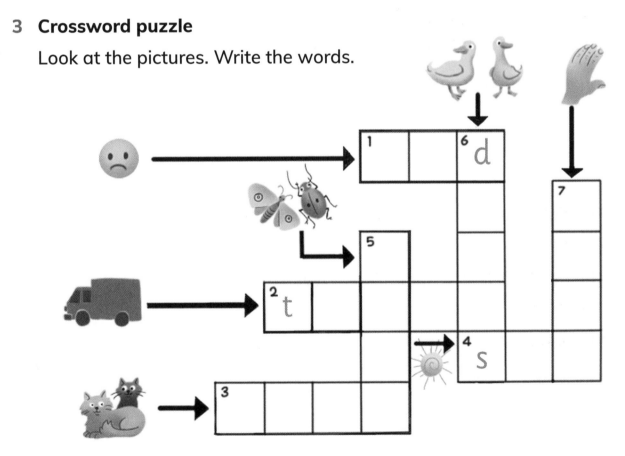

45 >

> 3.6 The Ker-PLUNK

1 Think about the story *The Ker-PLUNK*.

Read each sentence. Is it true? Circle yes or no.

a   The tree is next to the pond.   **yes   no**

b   Rabbit hears a strange sound.   **yes   no**

c   Rabbit is scared.   **yes   no**

d   There are three ducks.   **yes   no**

e   There are three frogs.   **yes   no**

f   The Ker-PLUNK is a big scary   **yes   no**
    animal.

g   The Ker-PLUNK is a nut falling   **yes   no**
    in the pond.

h   The lion is silly.   **yes   no**

i   The rabbit, ducks and frogs   **yes   no**
    are silly.

2 Write and draw.

Write a comic strip story about you and the silly Rabbit.

Why is Rabbit scared?

Write the missing word in the box and draw a picture in frame 2.

What can you say to Rabbit so he feels better?

Use sentences from the box or your own ideas.

It's OK, Rabbit.	Don't be scared, Rabbit.	I'm here with you.
A _____ is not scary.	Let's go look at it.	We can say 'hello'.

⟩ 3.7 Check your progress

Listen to your teacher. Tick (✔) the correct pictures.

Listen and write.

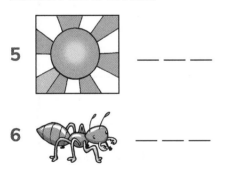

5 _ _ _ _

6 _ _ _ _

Read the sentences. Tick (✔) the correct pictures.

7   The man has a truck.

a

b

8   The duck runs.

a

b

Reflection

Talk with a partner.

1   What was your favourite activity in this unit?
    Circle one of these pictures or write a different answer.

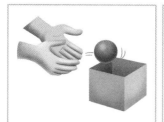
Make up a game with a ball and box.

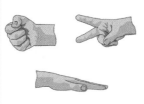
Play: *Rock, paper, scissors.*

Sing: *Wind the bobbin up.*

Act out a play: *The Ker-Plunk.*

_____

2   Which activity was the hardest? Draw a line under the picture.

3   Write 3 new words you learned.

_____   _____   _____

4 ▶ Making things

Colour in the stars as you learn to do each thing.

1 ☆ I can talk about what people are wearing and making.

2 ☆ I can talk about shapes.

3 ☆ I can count to 20.

4 ☆ I can talk and write about what people are making and doing.

5 ☆ I can read, talk about and act out a story.

> 4.1 What are they wearing?

1 Read, draw and colour.

Follow the instructions and colour the picture.

a I'm wearing yellow glasses.
 Colour the glasses yellow.

b And a bright blue skirt. Colour the skirt blue.

c I'm wearing a red shirt.
 Colour the shirt red.

d There's a diamond on my shirt.
 Colour the diamond yellow.

2 Unscramble the words.

The words in the box will help you.

dress	shirt	trousers	jacket
skirt	shoes	glasses	hat

 a trish _____

 e lssesga _____

 b ressd _____

 f kcajet _____

 c kirts _____

  g tha _____

 d sesho _____

 h rsoutsre _____

› 4.2 Making puppets

1 **What can you make out of old things?**

Brainstorm with your class or your partner.

Can you make pictures? Can you make puppets?

Your name _____	
What I can recycle	**Things I can make**
wrapping paper ———→	paper chain

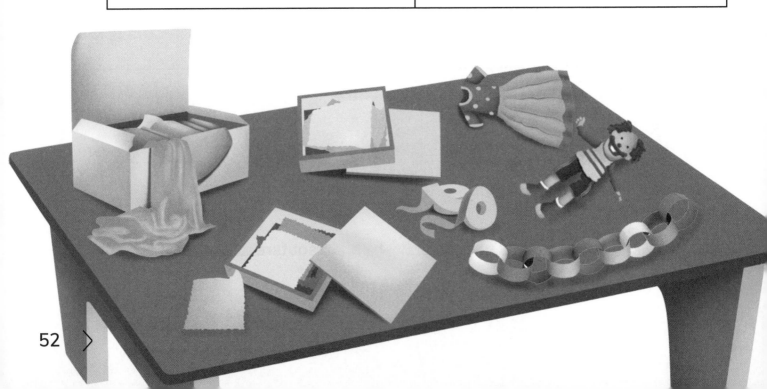

2 Draw and write.

What can you make?

Write two sentences. Draw a picture.

I can make _____ .

It has _____ .

3 Write the words.

Look at the picture of the puppets.

Use the words in the box to complete the sentences.

She's	They're	He's

_He's_ wearing a hat.   _____ wearing glasses.

_____ wearing shirts.

Challenge

Colour all of the clothing that the puppets are wearing.
Write sentences to describe what the puppets are wearing.

dress   shirt   trousers   jacket   skirt   shoes   glasses   hat

❯ 4.3 Colourful quilts with shapes

1 **Make a quilt.**

   Draw a shape in every square in the quilt below.

   You can draw a **triangle** △ , a **diamond** ◇ or a **rectangle** ▭ .

   Choose a colour from the box. Write the colours in the sentences.

   | red | blue | yellow | green |
   | orange | purple | black | pink |

   a The triangles are _____ .

   b The diamonds are _____ .

   c The rectangles are _____ .

   Now colour the shapes on your quilt.

2 Count the shapes on the clown.

Write the numbers.

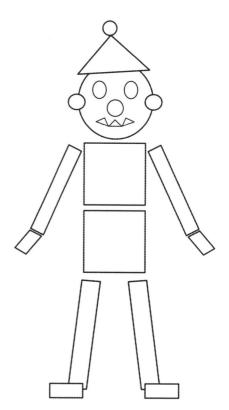

a How many squares are there? _____

b How many triangles are there? _____

c How many rectangles are there? _____

d How many circles are there? _____

3 Colour the shapes.

Read the sentences. Colour the clown.

The clown's hat is red.

The clown's arms are blue.

The clown's legs are orange.

4 What are they wearing?

Look at the pictures. What should these people be wearing?

Draw the clothes to complete the pictures.

Write sentences about the pictures.

warm coat	shorts	T-shirt	raincoat

He's at the seaside. He's wearing _____ .

She's in the rain. She's wearing _____ .

She's _____ .

〉 4.4 Painting a mural

Focus

1 Look at the pictures.

Complete the sentences using words from the box.

What are they doing?

a   He's ___playing___ football.

b   She's _____ a frog.

c   She's not _____ a quilt.

d   He's _____ a picture.

playing	painting
making	holding

What are they wearing?

a   She's holding a frog and she's ___wearing a skirt___.

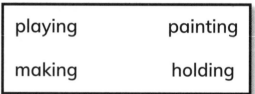

b   He's playing football and he's _____.

c   He's painting a picture and he's _____.

Practice

2 What are you wearing?

Describe what you are wearing.

3 **Complete the sentences.**

What is the boy wearing?

| dress | shirt | trousers | jacket |
| skirt | shoes | glasses | hat |

a He is wearing trousers.

b He _____ .

c He _____ .

What is the girl wearing?

a She is wearing a dress.

b She _____ .

c She _____ .

Challenge

4 **Write what the children are doing.**

Write sentences using words from the box.

| playing | cutting |
| making | wearing |

a They're _____ .

b _____ .

c _____ .

❭ 4.5 Short e

1 Write the words.

Look at the box. Write the short **e**, short **a** or short **u** words in the chart.

Words with short **e** sound	Words with short **a** sound	Words with short **u** sound

2 Find the words that rhyme.

Find two words that rhyme with **hen**. _____ _____

Find a word that rhymes with **bug**. _____

Find two words that rhyme with **can**. _____ _____

3 Make up a song.

Make up a new song like *London Bridge*.

Choose Grandma's **table**, **chair** or **car**. Colour it with two colours.
(The colour words are in Learner's Book page 13.)

Write the words to your song. Then sing your song with a friend.

We are painting Grandma's _____.

Grandma's _____, Grandma's _____.

We are painting Grandma's _____.

My fair lady.

We can paint it _____ and _____.

_____ and _____,

_____ and _____.

We can paint it _____ and _____.

My fair lady.

> 4.6 The Elves and the Shoemaker

1 What happens in the story?

Match the questions and answers.

a What is the title of the story?	• two
b How many elves are in the story?	• The Elves and the Shoemaker
c How do the elves help the shoemaker?	• They make shoes for him.
d How does the shoemaker help the elves?	• one
e How many shoemakers are in the story?	• He makes clothes for them.

2 New clothes!

Write the words on the labels. The box will help you.

jacket	trousers	hat	boots

3 Is it true?

Read each sentence. Circle **yes** or **no**.

a The shoemaker is tired.   **Yes   No**

b The shoemaker is making a shirt.   **Yes   No**

c The shoemaker is making shoes.   **Yes   No**

d The elves are sleeping.   **Yes   No**

4 A letter to the shoemaker.

Pretend you are one of the elves. Write a **thank you** letter to the shoemaker for the new clothes.

Challenge

Use some of these words in your letter:

lovely   new   beautiful   clothes   I like

Draw the elf in his new clothes.

Dear Shoemaker,
Thank you for the

_____

_____

_____

_____

Yours truly,
The Elves

❭ 4.7 Check your progress

Listen to your teacher. Tick (✔) the correct pictures.

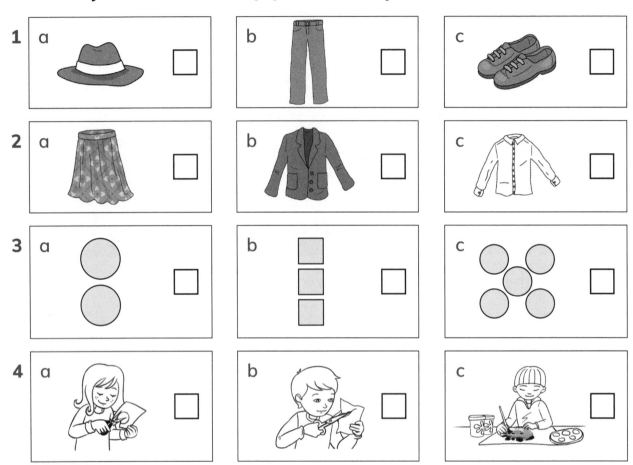

Write the words.

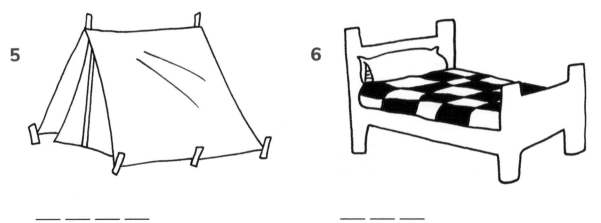

5 _ _ _ _ _

6 _ _ _

Read the sentences. Tick (✔) the correct pictures.

7 The hen has ten eggs.

a

b

8 Meg is wearing a dress.

a

b

Reflection

Talk with a partner.

1 What was your favourite learning activity in this unit?

Tick (✔) one of these answers or write a different answer.

☐ singing songs   ☐ making puppets

☐ talking about shapes   ☐ reading stories

☐ talking about what people are wearing

2 Write 3 new words you learned.

_____ _____ _____

5 On the farm

Colour in the stars as you learn to do each thing.

1. I can name things on a farm.

2. I can talk about what people are doing.

3. I can learn about how plants and animals grow and change.

4. I can ask and answer questions.

5. I can read and write words with short **i**.

6. I can read, talk about and act out a story.

＞ 5.1 What can you find on a farm?

1 It's time to feed the animals!

Write a sentence for each picture.

The box and *Writing tip* will help you.

hen   lamb   horse

a

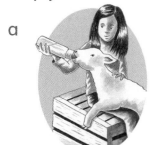

She is feeding the lamb.

b

c

Writing tip

He is feeding the animals.

She is feeding the animals.

They are feeding the animals.

> 5.2 Living on a farm

1 Find the matching picture.

a planting

b picking

c driving

d feeding

e carrying

2 Write the sentences.

a

He _____.

b

_____ are _____.

Language detective

If you are talking about 1 person , do you use **is** or **are**?

If you are talking about 2 people 👤👤, do you use **am** or **are**?

3 Draw a circle around the living things.

Living things need food and water to grow.
Which of these are living things?

Name two other living things.

_____   _____

Challenge

Draw a picture of yourself helping on a farm. What are you doing?
Write a sentence.

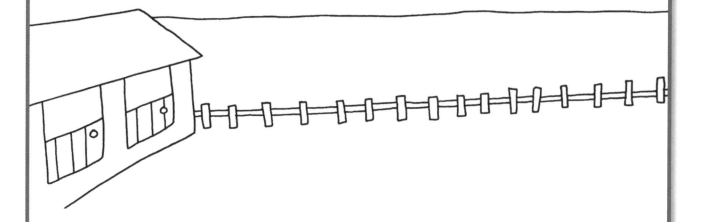

_____

_____

> 5.3 Life cycles

1 (Circle) the three animals that lay eggs.

turtle   hen   cow   fish   lion

Challenge

Name the two animals that lay eggs and can swim.

_____ and _____ .

2 **Baby animals**

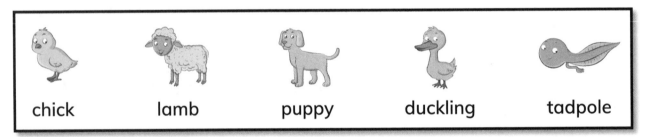

chick   lamb   puppy   duckling   tadpole

a A _____ is a baby sheep.

b A _____ is a baby hen.

c A _____ is a baby dog.

d A _____ is a baby frog.

e A _____ is a baby duck.

3 Life cycle of a duck

Complete the life cycle sentences and pictures.

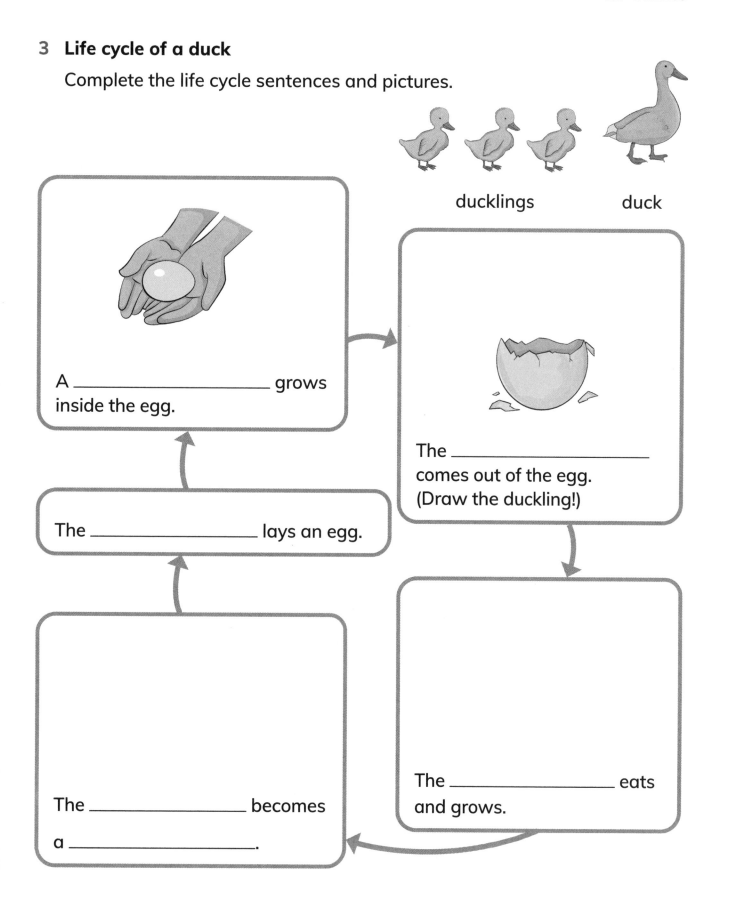

ducklings   duck

A _____ grows inside the egg.

The _____ comes out of the egg. (Draw the duckling!)

The _____ lays an egg.

The _____ eats and grows.

The _____ becomes a _____.

〉 5.4 What is happening on the farm?

Focus

1 Look and point.

What are the animals doing?

What is the hen doing?

2 Look at the picture and complete the sentences.

Use the words in the box to complete the sentences.

a The hen _____is carrying_____ eggs.

b The chicks _____ the seeds.

c The cow _____ the tractor.

d The goats _____ strawberries.

| driving |
| carrying |
| picking |
| eating |

3 What else is happening at the farm?

Look at the picture. In pairs, talk about what else you can see.

Practice

4 Answer the questions.

a Write 'Yes, *it is*' or 'No, *it is not*' to answer.

- Is the goat standing on one leg? _____

- Is it using a computer? _____

b How about you? Write 'Yes , *I am*' or 'No, *I am not*'.

- Are you standing on one leg? _____

- Are you writing with a pencil? _____

5 What is the family doing?

Complete the sentences using words from the box.

using	dinner
cooking	a game
playing	TV
watching	the computer

a The grandpa is _____.

b The sisters are _____.

c The grandma is _____.

d The brother is _____.

Challenge

6 What are you doing right now?

I am _____.

> 5.5 Short i

1 Read and draw.

a Draw six pink fish.

b Draw a red bug on the stick.

c Draw a big stick.

d Draw a chick on the ship.

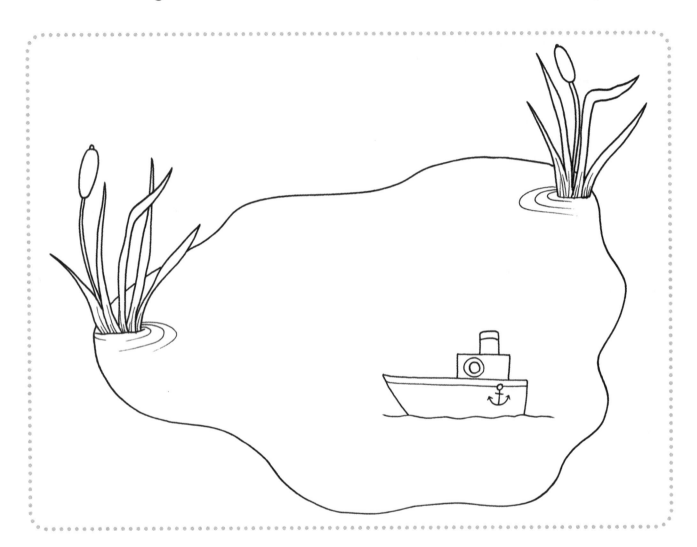

Look at your partner's picture. Ask questions.

2 Rhyming words

Rhyming words end with the same sound,
like **sheep** and **sleep**.

Draw a line between the words that rhyme.

stick

duck

truck

swing

ring

chick

Challenge

Write 2 more words
that rhyme with **ring**.

_____

_____

3 Animal crossword puzzle

Look at the small pictures.
Write the words.

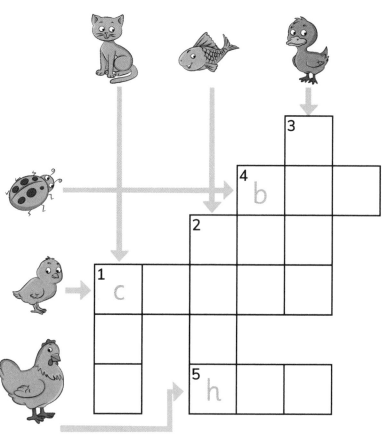

> 5.6 *The Little Red Hen*

1 Is it true?

Look at the pictures. Read the sentences. (Circle) **yes** or **no**.

a    Little Red Hen is talking to Duck.   **yes**   **no**

b    Bird is helping Little Red Hen.   **yes**   **no**

c    Chick and Duck are helping.   **yes**   **no**

d   The bread is delicious.   **yes**   **no**

e   Little Red Hen is sad.   **yes**   **no**

2 Favourite character.

Who's your favourite character?
Circle your answer.

Ask a friend, 'Who's your
favourite character?'

Little Red Hen   Chick   Duck

Write the answer: _____

Do you and your friend have the same favourite character?

Circle **yes** or **no**.   **yes**   **no**

3 Thank you!

Write a thank you card for a friend, a teacher or someone in your family.

The box has some things you can write:

Thank you for helping me.	Thank you for being my friend.
Thank you for playing with me.	Thank you for fixing my toy.
Thank you for reading with me.	

Dear _____

_____

_____

_____

_____

_____

_____

_____

⟩ 5.7 Check your progress

Listen to your teacher. Tick (✔) the correct pictures.

1
a  ☐
b  ☐
c  ☐

2
a  ☐
b  ☐
c  ☐

3
a  ☐
b  ☐
c  ☐

4
a  ☐
b  ☐
c  ☐

Listen and write.

5 | 6 | 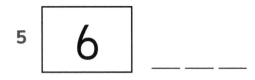 __ __ __

6  __ __ __ __

Read the sentences. Tick (✔) the correct pictures.

7 The hen is eating.

a
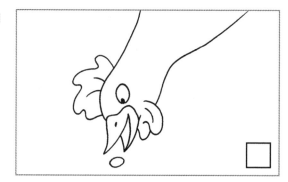

b
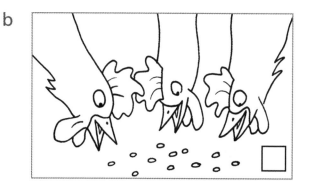

8 The ducks are swimming.

a

b

Reflection

Talk with a partner

1 What was your favourite learning activity in this unit?

_____

2 Which activity was the hardest?

_____

3 Write 3 new words you learned.

_____   _____   _____

6 My five senses

Colour in the stars as you learn to do each thing.

1. I can name the five senses.

2. I can talk about sounds.

3. I can use senses to describe things.

4. I can read and write words with short o.

5. I can listen to, read and act out a story.

> 6.1 How do we use our five senses?

1 Read and write.

Read the sentences about senses and write the missing words.
The words are in the box.

| hear | taste | see | touch | smell |

a I _____ with my eyes.

b I _____ with my ears.

c I _____ with my nose.

d I _____ with my mouth.

e I _____ with my hand.

Challenge

Look around you. What can you **see**?

I can see _____.

Listen to the sounds around you. What can you **hear**?

_____

Think of some things that taste good. Which taste do you like best?

I like the taste of _____.

› 6.2 What do you hear?

1 Animal band

Write about the animals and the instruments they are playing.

drum

piano

saxophone

triangle

violin

The cow is playing the _____.

Two ducks _____.

A sheep _____.

Two cats _____.

A little chick _____.

2 What can you play?

(Circle) your answer.

Can you play the triangle?	Yes, I can.	No, I can't.
Can you play the saxophone?	Yes, I can.	No, I can't.
Can you play the drum?	Yes, I can.	No, I can't.

3 **Experiment: Three drums**

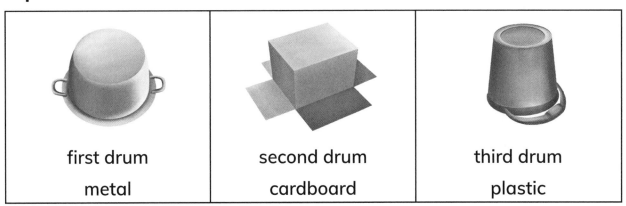

first drum	second drum	third drum
metal	cardboard	plastic

a Which drum is louder, the first drum or the second drum?

_____

b Which drum is louder, the first drum or the third drum?

_____

c Which drum makes your favourite sound?

_____

Challenge

Find something in your classroom that is made of **metal** or **plastic**. Draw a picture.

This is made of _____.

4 **My favourite sound**

Think of all the sounds you can hear. What's your favourite sound?

Write a sentence.

My favourite sound is _____

_____.

〉 6.3 Using your five senses

1 Colour and write.

Do you like these smells? Colour or .

Write Yes, *I do.* or No, *I don't.*

a  flowers

 _____

b  fish

 _____

c  soap

 _____

d  bananas

 _____

e  smoke

 _____

f soup

 _____

Challenge

Write one other smell that you like.

Write one other smell that you **don't** like.

(Tip: Look at the *Picture Dictionary* for ideas.)

I like the smell of _____.

I don't like the smell of _____.

2 Describe how objects feel.

How do the objects feel when you touch them?
Choose 3 words for each object from the box.

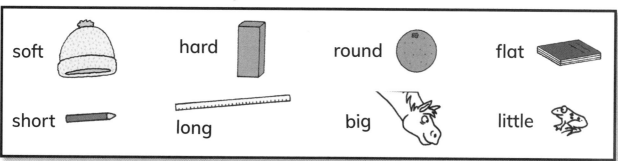

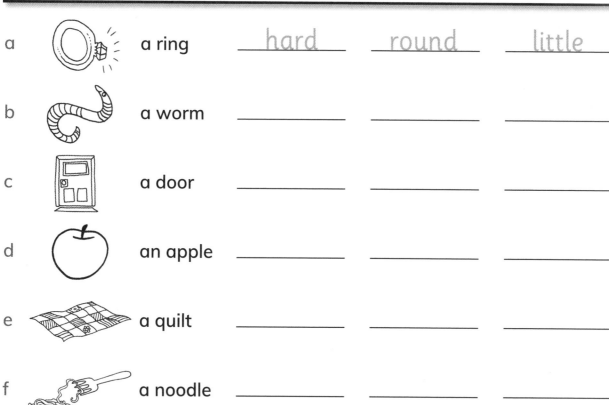

a a ring _hard_ _round_ _little_

b a worm _____ _____ _____

c a door _____ _____ _____

d an apple _____ _____ _____

e a quilt _____ _____ _____

f a noodle _____ _____ _____

Challenge

Draw something that is little and soft.
Write the word.

_____

> 6.4 Sweet and loud

Focus

1 Which instrument is being described?

Look at the instruments. (Circle) the one that is being described.

a This drum is loud. b This piano is big. c This saxophone is long.

2 Complete the sentences.

Look at the picture. Fill in the missing words to describe the instruments.

This drum is ___loud___ .   This drum is ___soft___ .

This saxophone

is _____.

This piano is

_____.

This piano is _____.   This saxophone is _____.

3 **Compare with your senses.**

Write something that is ...

sweet: _____ *sweets* _____ .

salty: _____ *popcorn* _____ .

round: _____ .

flat: _____ .

hot: _____ .

cold: _____ .

hard: _____ .

soft: _____ .

Challenge

Challenge your friend.

Think about the sentences below. Write your answers and compare them with a friend.

a Write three things you can see right now.

1 ___ *my book* ___ 2 _____ 3 _____

b Write two things you can hear right now.

1 _____ 2 _____

c Write one thing you can smell right now.

1 _____

d Write three things you can touch right now.

1 ___ *my book* ___ 2 _____ 3 _____

e Write one salty food and one sweet food that you want to taste right now.

1 _____ 2 _____

> 6.5 Short o

1 Word snake

Find these words in the Word snake. (Circle) them.

Then write the words next to the pictures.
Underline the short o sound in each word.

a 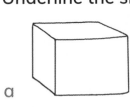 box

f _____

b  _____

g  _____

c  _____

h  _____

d  _____

i  _____

e  _____

j  _____

as (box) pthfrogpondsockprgpotarrfoxdogclockjsrockqulog

2 **Tick, tock, hop!**

Read the story again in the Learner's Book (page 109).

Then read the questions. (Circle) the answers.

a   What makes the sound Tick tock. Tick tock?

the pond   a clock

b   Who hits a rock with two sticks?

Bob the frog   Fred the fox

c   What makes the sound Flip, flop. Flip, flop?

the fish in the pond   a clock on a rock

d   Which animals can hop?

the fish and the fox   the rabbits and the frog

3 **Read and colour.**

Follow the instructions under the picture.

Colour the pond blue.   Colour the fox orange.
Colour the frog green.   Colour the log brown.
Colour the clock yellow.   Colour the rock grey.

〉 6.6 Five Friends and the Elephant

1 Parts of the elephant

Look at the picture of the elephant.

Write the correct words on the lines.

leg   trunk   side   tail   ear

a _____ b _____ c _____ d _____ e _____

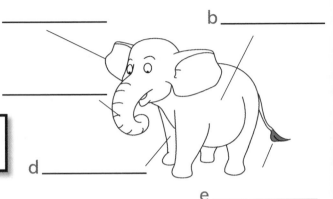

2 Read and colour.

Five elephants are walking together. Read the sentences. Follow the instructions.

Colour the third elephant yellow. Colour its ears orange.

Colour the fourth elephant grey. Colour its tail red.

Colour the fifth elephant pink. Colour its trunk purple.

Colour the second elephant brown. Colour its legs green.

Colour the first elephant blue. Draw a hat on its head.

3   Write: Five friends meet a deer.

The five blind friends meet a deer.

Each friend touches a different part of the deer and says how it feels.

What does each friend say? Write the words in the speech bubbles.

Look at the box for some ideas.

long	thin	soft	hard	furry	wiggly

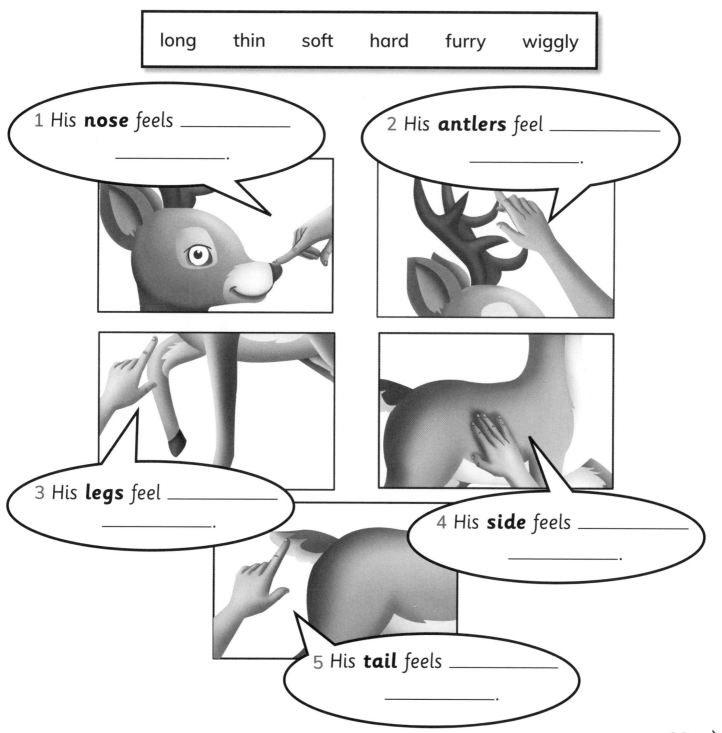

1 His **nose** feels _____ _____ .

2 His **antlers** feel _____ _____ .

3 His **legs** feel _____ _____ .

4 His **side** feels _____ _____ .

5 His **tail** feels _____ _____ .

❭ 6.7 Check your progress

Listen to your teacher. Tick (✔) the correct pictures.

1
a  ☐
b 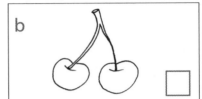 ☐
c 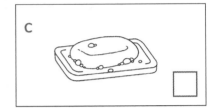 ☐

2
a 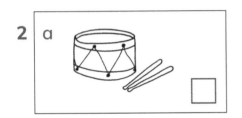 ☐
b 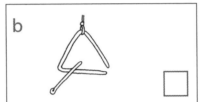 ☐
c  ☐

3
a 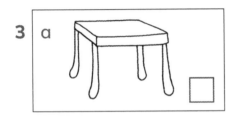 ☐
b  ☐
c  ☐

4
a  ☐
b  ☐
c  ☐

Listen and write.

5 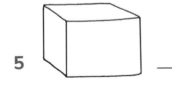 _ _ _ _ _

6  _ _ _ _ _

Read the sentences. Tick (✔) the correct pictures.

7 The boy is tall.

a

☐

b

☐

8 The fox sits on the log.

a

☐

b

☐

Reflection

Talk with a partner.

1 What are you good at?

☐ listening to and understanding English

☐ talking in English

☐ singing in English

☐ reading in English

☐ writing in English

2 What would you like more help with?

☐ listening to and understanding English

☐ talking in English

☐ reading in English

☐ writing in English

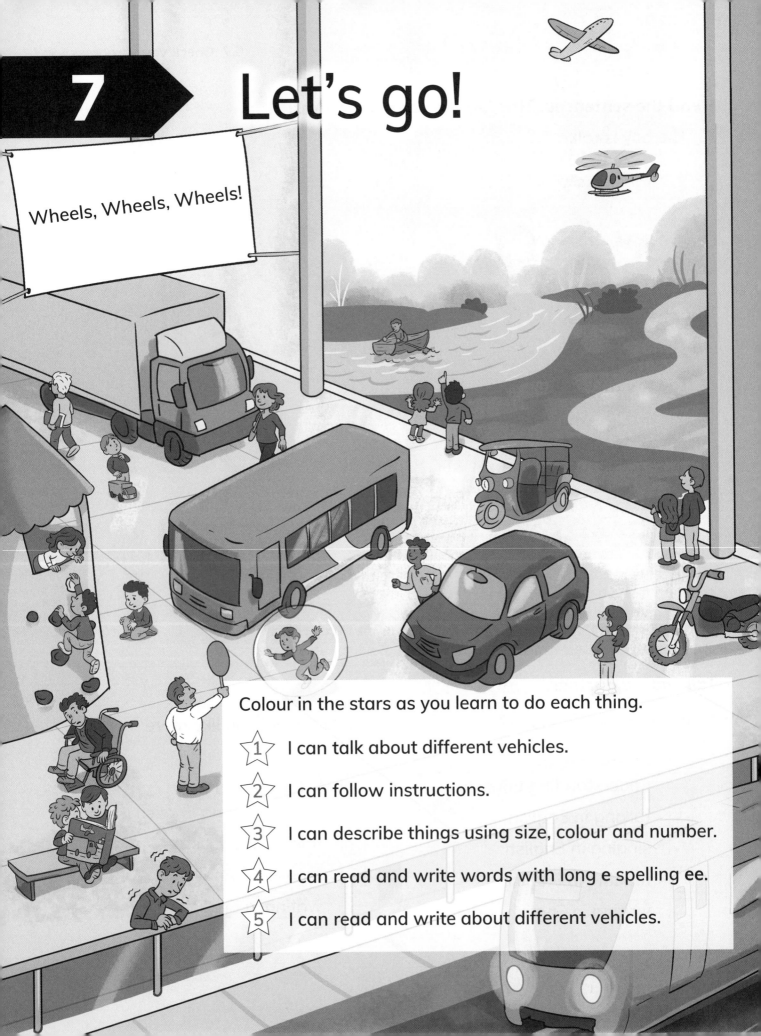

7 ▶ Let's go!

Wheels, Wheels, Wheels!

Colour in the stars as you learn to do each thing.

1. I can talk about different vehicles.

2. I can follow instructions.

3. I can describe things using size, colour and number.

4. I can read and write words with long e spelling ee.

5. I can read and write about different vehicles.

❭ 7.1 How do we travel around?

1 Rides at Fun Land

Complete the sign for each ride.

Use words from the box.

fly	climb	float
	drive	slide

a _____ down the slide!

b _____ down the river!

c _____ a car!

d _____ up the tower!

e _____ in a plane!

2 Draw and write.

Draw a picture of you on a ride at Fun Land.

Write a sentence about it.

I can _____ _____ a _____ .

> 7.2 Vehicles

1 What is your favourite vehicle?

Write a sentence and draw a picture.

My favourite vehicle is

_____ .

2 What is your friend's favourite vehicle?

Write their answer.

My friend's favourite

vehicle is _____ .

Do you and your friend have the same favourite way to move?

Circle **Yes** or **No.**   Yes   No

3 Different ways Alaskan children get to school.

What are three different vehicles that Alaskan children use
to get to school?

a _____

b _____

c _____

Is it easier to travel in the winter or in the summer? Why?

_____

_____

4 Read and colour.

Follow the instructions and colour the picture.

Colour the helicopter yellow.

Draw a green plane flying in the sky.

Draw a brown cat climbing up the tree.

Draw a boy on the slide. He is wearing a blue jacket.

Draw a girl on the swing. She is wearing a hat.

Challenge

Make up a name for the yellow helicopter. _____

Make up a name for the green plane. _____

> 7.3 Make a helicopter and a plane

1 Race the helicopters.

Have a helicopter race with two classmates.

Which helicopter stayed up for longer?

	Helicopter 1	Helicopter 2	Helicopter 3
Trial 1			
Trial 2			
Trial 3			
Trial 4			

2 Race the planes.

Have a plane race with two classmates.

Which plane flew further?

	Plane 1	Plane 2	Plane 3
Trial 1			
Trial 2			
Trial 3			
Trial 4			

Challenge

Why did the plane fly further?

_____

3 Out of my window

What vehicles can you see out of the window?

Circle and colour the vehicles you can see.

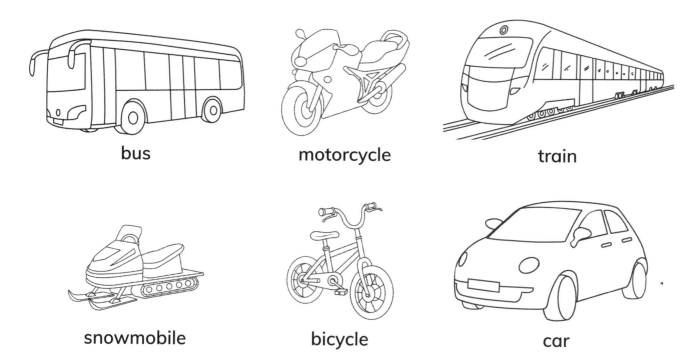

bus   motorcycle   train

snowmobile   bicycle   car

4 Which order?

Think of some vehicles. Can you describe them?

Add the missing number, size, colour or vehicle words to complete each sentence.

	number word	size	colour	vehicle
I see	three	big	red	snowmobiles.
I see	two			
I see		small		
I see			green	
I see				bike.

› 7.4 Describing things

Focus

1 Look at the pictures below.

Colour each type of vehicle in a different colour. Complete the sentences.

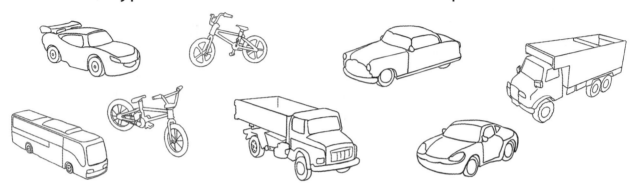

There is one ___small___ ___black___ car.

There are two ___big___ _____ cars.

There are two ___small___ _____ trucks.

There is one _____ _____ bus.

There are two _____ _____ bicycles.

Practice

2 Colour the balls.

Make sentences about the balls.

1 There is
_____
_____ .

2 There are _____
_____ .

3 Complete the table.

Look at the vehicles. There are some shapes missing.
Draw along the dotted lines to complete the shapes.

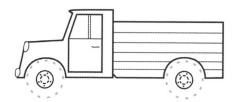  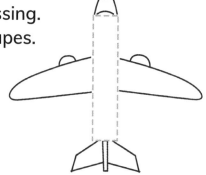

Look at the table. Which colour is each vehicle?
Colour the vehicles then complete the table.

Vehicle	Size?	Colour?	Shape?
truck	big	red	circle
boat	small	blue	
plane		yellow	

Challenge

4 Complete and colour the truck.

Write a sentence to describe the truck.

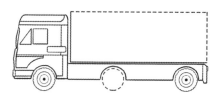 It is a big green truck. It has

_____

_____

〉 7.5 Long e spelling ee

1 What's in the picture?

Write the words on the labels.
The box will help you.

teeth	seeds	bees
knees	tree	Jeep
a sleeping sheep		wheel

3 _____

2 _____

4 _____

1 _____

6 _____

7 _____

8 _____

5 _____

2 How many?

Look at the picture. Answer the questions with one word.

a How many wheels can you see? _____

b How many sheep are there? _____

c How many bees are there? _____

3 Rhyme

In each box, (circle) the two words that rhyme.

a

b

Challenge

Can you think of a word that rhymes with each of these words?

seed _____   feel _____   Jeep _____

4 Word snake

Look at the Word snake. (Circle) all of the words with **ee**.

Look at the pictures.

Which picture word is not in the word snake? _____

 ghkneeckeeprsfeedbaagbseobeeheppabeepwheelyetdeersleepo

> 7.6 Travelling around

1 Name the vehicle.

Look at the pictures. Put the letters in the correct order to make the word.

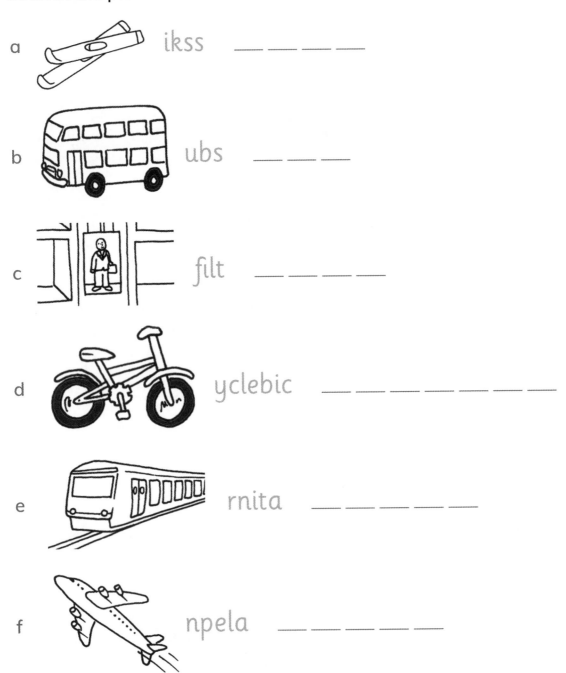

a ikss _ _ _ _

b ubs _ _ _

c filt _ _ _ _

d yclebic _ _ _ _ _ _ _

e rnita _ _ _ _ _

f npela _ _ _ _ _

2 Which vehicles have you travelled in? Circle the pictures.

3 Make a sea picture postcard.

Choose a different colour for each thing.
Then colour the picture.

The sea is ___blue___ .

The big boat is _____ .

The sails on the big boat are

_____ .

The little boat is _____ .

The sail on the little boat

_____ .

4 Write your postcard.

Postcard

Dear _____ ,

I am at the seaside.

Look at the big _____ boat.

It has _____

_____ sails.

Wish you were here!

From,

_____

_____

_____

_____

❯ 7.7 Check your progress

Listen to your teacher. Tick (✔) the correct pictures.

Read the words. Draw lines to the matching pictures.

5 bee

6 Jeep

7 teeth

8 tree

Read the sentences. Tick (✔) the correct pictures.

9 The bee is under the tree.

a

☐

b

☐

10 The bus is small.

a

☐

b

☐

Reflection

Talk with a partner.

1 What is your favourite thing to do in English class?

☐ talk about different vehicles   ☐ read and write **ee** words

☐ follow instructions   ☐ read and write about vehicles

☐ learn about real things

Look back at the unit.

2 What do you think is the most interesting way to move?

_____

3 What do you think is the most interesting vehicle in the unit?

_____

105 〉

8 City places

Colour in the stars as you learn to do each new thing.

1 I can talk and read about things in a city.

2 I can describe and ask questions using *this* and *these*.

3 I can read and write words that end in –y.

4 I can name opposites.

5 I can read and talk about a poem.

> 8.1 What can you see, hear and do?

1 Read, draw and colour.

Follow the instructions under the picture.

a   The traffic lights say STOP! Colour the light on top red.

b   A blue car stops at the traffic lights. Draw the blue car on the road.

c   A girl is waiting for a bus. Draw the girl at the bus stop.

d   A boy is looking at the bike shop.
   Draw the boy on the pavement next to the shop.

> 8.2 Around the city

1 What can you hear and see in a city?

Brainstorm with your class or your partner.

Write the name of your city or town. Make two lists.

The name of my city is _____

In the city, I can hear	In the city, I can see
_____	_____
_____	_____
_____	_____
_____	_____

2 Write and draw.

Write two sentences. Draw a picture.

In _____,
(name of your city)

I can hear _____ and

_____.

I can see _____ and

_____.

3 Draw and talk about patterns.

a   Look at these tall and short trees along a city street.

Talk with your partner about the pattern.

What is next? Draw the 8th, 9th and 10th tree.

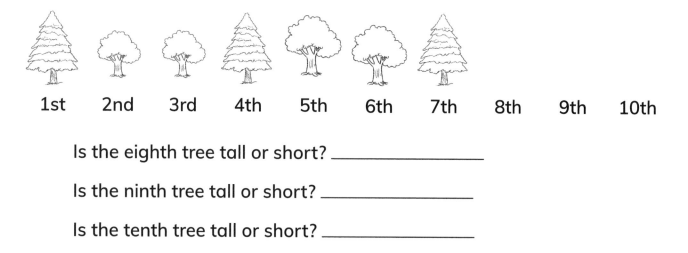

1st   2nd   3rd   4th   5th   6th   7th   8th   9th   10th

Is the eighth tree tall or short? _____

Is the ninth tree tall or short? _____

Is the tenth tree tall or short? _____

b   Use a red crayon and a blue crayon to colour these 10 cars in a pattern.

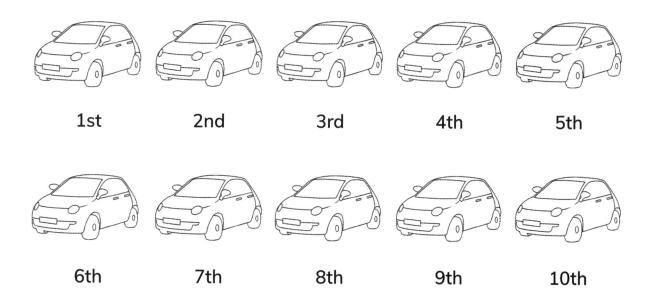

1st   2nd   3rd   4th   5th

6th   7th   8th   9th   10th

What colour is your first car? _____

What colour is your second car? _____

What colour is your third car? _____

> 8.3 City living

1 City places

Look at the pictures. Write the letters in the correct order.

a

p r a k ___ ___ ___ ___

b

d r o a ___ ___ ___ ___

c

o z o ___ ___ ___

2 Places near your home

Which of the places above are near your home? Write the words.

_____

Challenge

What other things or places can you see near your home?
(Tip: Look at the *Picture dictionary* on Learner's Book page 175 for ideas.)

_____   _____

3 **Let's buy an ice cream!**

Look at the picture.
The ice cream seller and the girl are talking.

Write the missing words on the lines.
They are in the box.

Write your favourite flavour in the second speech bubble.

here
thank you
please
small

Hi! I'd like to buy an ice cream, _____.

Sure! What flavour?

A _____ ice cream, please.

Big or _____?

Big!

_____ you are.

_____
_____!

Challenge

Read the clues. Can you find the mystery words?
They are in the Learner's Book (page 138).

1 Put your litter in this. b ____ ____

2 You can find this in a park. Fish live in it. p ____ ____ ____

3 These can be tall or short. They have windows and doors.

b ____ ____ ____ ____ ____ ____ ____

〉 8.4 This or these?

Focus

1 **Look at the picture and complete the sentences.**

Use the words from the box.

This baby is _____.

| happy | noisy | crying |

This baby is _____.

These babies are _____.

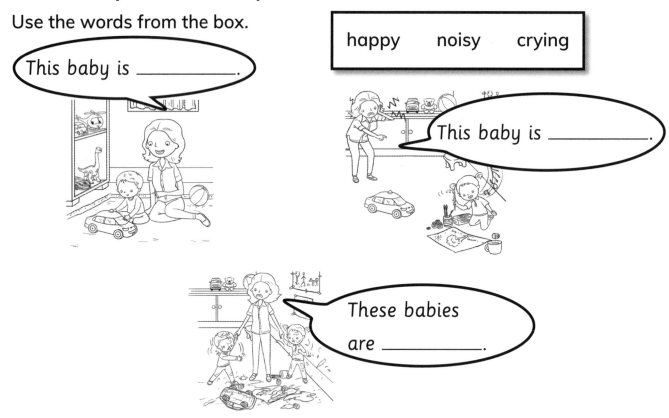

2 **Look at the picture. (Circle) the correct answer for each question.**

Use the words from the box.

What is this?

What is that?

What are these?

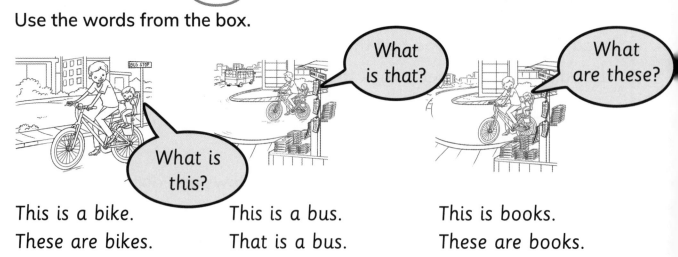

This is a bike.   This is a bus.   This is books.
These are bikes.   That is a bus.   These are books.

Practice

3 This or these?

Complete the sentences below. Write *This is* or *These are*.

a <u>This</u> <u>is</u> <u>a</u> ball.

b <u>These</u> <u>are</u> zebras.

c _____ _____ rabbits.

d _____ _____ <u>a</u> car.

e _____ _____ <u>a</u> pavement.

f _____ _____ buses.

Challenge

4 Draw and ask.

Draw a picture and then write a question about your picture.

Ask your partner to answer the question.

a What are _____?

b What is _____?

c What _____?

> 8.5 –y endings

1 Which –y sound?

fly	baby
In some of these words, the –**y** sounds like the long **i**: **fly**	In some of these words, the –**y** sounds like the long **e**: **baby**
_____ _____ _____	_____ _____ _____

Write the words from the box in the correct column.

city   cry   scary   sky   bakery

Challenge

Look at these words from the song *I live in a city*.

1 Circle 3 words with the letter **y**.

I live in a city, yes I do,
Made by human hands.

Write the words here: _____ _____ _____

2 Say the words. Is **y** the same or a different sound?
Circle **same** or **different**.

2 Opposites crossword

Read the clues and write the answers in the crossword puzzle.

All the answers are in the *box*.

| big | stop | bad | noisy | hot | new | down | happy |

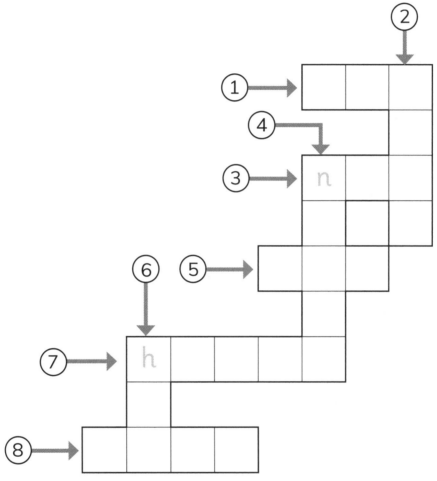

① → The opposite of **good**.

② ↓ The opposite of **up**.

③ → The opposite of **old**.

④ ↓ The opposite of **quiet**.

⑤ → The opposite of **small**.

⑥ ↓ The opposite of **cold**.

⑦ → The opposite of **sad**.

⑧ → The opposite of **go**.

> 8.6 *Sing a Song of People*

1 **Sing a song of people.**

Write the missing word at the end of each verse.

Clue: The word rhymes with the last word in the second line (in **bold**).

People on the sidewalk,

People on the **bus**;

People passing, passing,

In back and front of _____.

a

People on the subway

Underneath the **ground**;

People riding taxis

Round and round and _____.

b

People in tall buildings

And in stores **below**;

Riding elevators

Up and down they _____.

c

People laughing, smiling,

Grumpy people **too**;

People who just hurry

And never look at _____!

d

2 **Match the pictures.**

Draw a line from the verse to the correct picture.

3 Vehicles in the city

What vehicles can you see?

Write the words below.

For help with spelling, look at the *Picture dictionary* in the Learner's Book (page 175).

_____   _____

4 Where is the goose?

Look at each picture.
Write a sentence to say where the goose is.

in	next to	on

The words in the box will help you.

a   The goose is _____ .

b   _____

c   _____

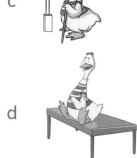

d   _____

› 8.7 Check your progress

Listen to your teacher. Tick (✔) the correct pictures.

1 a  b  c

2 a  b  c

3 a 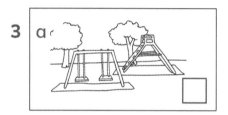 b  c

4 a  b  c

Listen and write.

5  _____ _____ _____

6  _____ _____ _____ _____

Read the sentences. Tick (✔) the correct pictures.

7 This ice cream is big.

a ☐

b ☐

8 This girl is happy.

a ☐

b ☐

Reflection

Talk with a partner.

1 What was your favourite learning activity in this unit?

Tick (✔) one of these answers or write a different answer.

☐ Learning about patterns

☐ Acting out a conversation

☐ Playing a game with a partner

☐ Singing 'I live in a city'

☐ Saying and acting out the 'Opposites' poem

☐ _____

2 Write 3 new words you learned in this unit.

_____ _____ _____

Colour in the stars as you learn to do each new thing.

What can you do today.
- Get wet!
- Walk in the wind.
- Sit on a cloud.
- Float a boat.
- Watch a play.
- Have fun!

1 I can talk about the weather.

2 I can talk about things we do every day.

3 I can say why plants, animals and people need water.

4 I can do experiments with things that float and don't float.

5 I can read and write words with the long **a** spellings **ay** and **ai**.

6 I can read, discuss and act out a play.

> 9.1 Why is water important?

1 Look at the pictures.

Write the letters in the correct order to make the weather words.

 a   y d n i w   _____

 b   y r a i n   _____

 c   n n y s u   _____

 d   o w y s n   _____

2 Look out the window.

What's the weather like today?

It's _____.

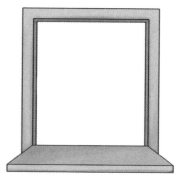

> 9.2 Day by day

1 Don't forget! Look at the picture. What does the girl need?

Choose one thing from the box and draw it in each picture.

| umbrella | sun hat | scarf and gloves |

It is raining.
The girl needs an
umbrella.

It is sunny.
The girl needs a
_____.

It is cold.
The girl needs a
_____.

2 Days of the week

Write the missing days.

Monday   Wednesday   Friday   Sunday

3 What do you do each day?

What do you do on Monday?

On Monday, I _____.

What do you do on Friday?

_____.

Monday

Friday

4 Write a rainy-day poem.

Choose words from the box or from the *Picture dictionary* in the Learner's Book (page 174).

cars   flowers   garden   window

pond   umbrellas

Rain on the _____.

Rain on the tree.

Rain on the _____.

And rain on me!

Draw a picture of your poem.

> 9.3 Facts about water

1 Which are the living things?

Animals and plants are living things. (Circle) the pictures of living things.

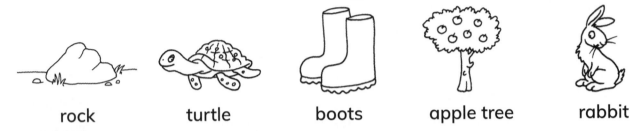

rock   turtle   boots   apple tree   rabbit

2 Draw and write.

Draw pictures of three more living things.
Write the words under the pictures.

3 Watery words!

Find these words in the Word snake. (Circle) the words.

rain   snow   river   lake   water   drink

4 Label the diagram.

Write the words on the lines. (The words in the *Word snake* will help you.)

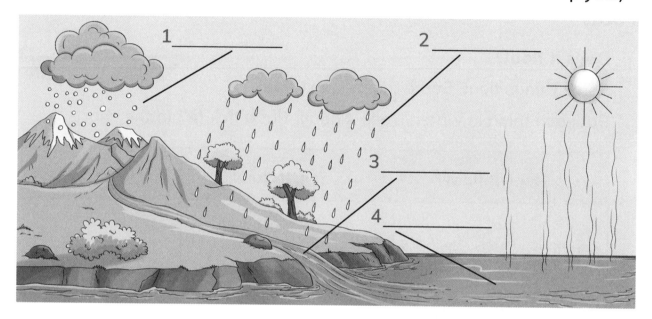

1 _____   2 _____

3 _____

4 _____

5 Over to you

Answer the questions with **Yes, there is.** or **No, there isn't.**

a Is there rain where you live? _____

b Is there snow where you live? _____

c Is there a river or lake near your house? _____

6 How do we use water?

Finish the two sentences. The box will give you some ideas.

tea	rice	clothes	bowls

a We use water to wash _____.

b We use water to make _____.

> 9.4 Things that float

Focus

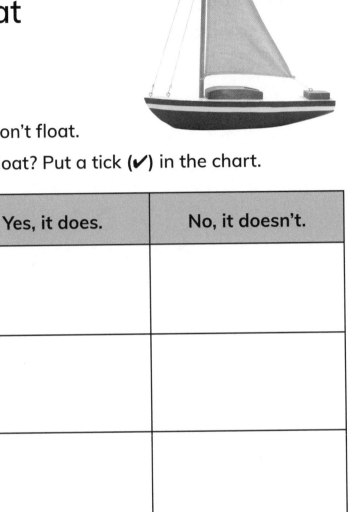

1 Does it float?

Some things float. Some things don't float.

Put each thing in water. Does it float? Put a tick (✔) in the chart.

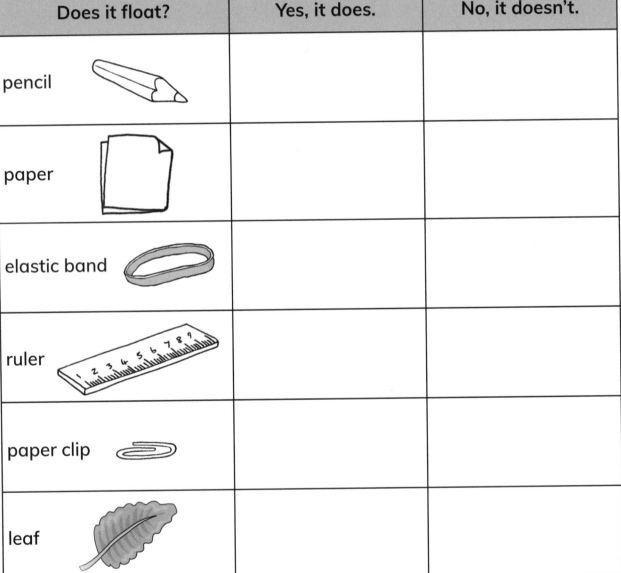

Does it float?	Yes, it does.	No, it doesn't.
pencil		
paper		
elastic band		
ruler		
paper clip		
leaf		

Practice

2   **Write about it.**

What floats? Choose two things. Write a sentence about each.

a   The _____ floats.

b   _____

What doesn't float? Choose two things. Write a sentence about each.

a   The _____ doesn't float.

b   _____

Challenge

3   **Don't forget!**

Look at the picture. The girl has forgotten something.

a   Choose one thing from the box and draw it in Mum's hand.

b   What is Mum saying? Write the words in the speech bubble.

ball   umbrella

boots   teddy

Don't forget your _____!

Yes, Mum!

› 9.5 Long **a** spellings **ai** and **ay**

1 Read and draw.

Follow the instructions under the image.

Circle the words with **ai**. Underline the words with **ay**.

a   The goose is painting. Colour the paint pot blue.

b   The boat on the sea has a sail. Colour the sail red.

c   Draw a snail next to the goose. Colour the snail green.

d   It's a sunny day. Draw the sun.

e   Two rabbits are playing with a ball. Draw the ball.

2 Rhyming words.

Write the rhyming words.

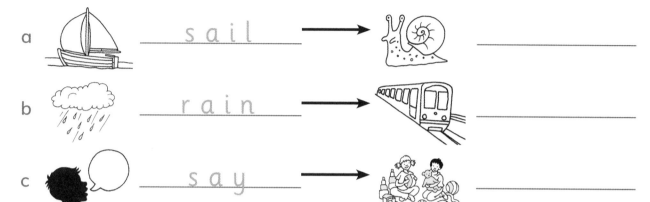

a   s a i l → _____

b   r a i n → _____

c   s a y → _____

3 Make a sentence.

Write a sentence with one of the words above.

Draw a picture to go with your sentence.

_____

_____

_____

Challenge

Write a sentence with **two** of the words above.

_____

_____

〉 9.6 The Song of the Toad

1 The Song of the Toad

What happens in the story? Read and put the pictures in the correct order.

Write the numbers 1–5 in the boxes.

Toad asks the Emperor to send rain.

It is very dry. The plants and the animals need water.

The Emperor sends rain to the earth.

Toad and his friends go to the Emperor in the castle.

Now Toad sings when the earth is dry. The farmers are happy. They know that rain will come soon.

Challenge

Why do the animals need rain?

_____

_____

2 **What do the characters say?**

What do the Guards say? What does the Emperor say?

Write a sentence with an exclamation mark in each speech bubble.

3 **Draw and write.**

Draw a picture of your favourite part of the story.

Add a speech bubble ⬭. Write what the character is saying.

❯ 9.7 Check your progress

Listen to your teacher. Tick (✔) the correct pictures.

1
a  □
b  □
c 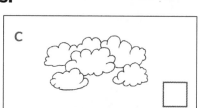 □

2
a  □
b  □
c  □

3
a 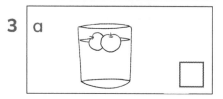 □
b 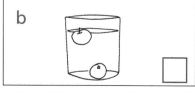 □
c  □

4
a  □
b 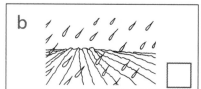 □
c  □

Listen, write and draw.

5 Write the missing word.

We can _ _ _ _ _ with a ball.

6 Listen and write. Draw a picture of the word.

_ _ _ _ _

Read the sentences. Tick (✔) the correct pictures.

7   The snails are playing.

a    ☐

b    ☐

8   I can paint a train.

a    ☐

b    ☐

Reflection

Talk with a partner.

1   What is your favourite thing to do in English class?

Tick (✔) one of these answers.

☐ talk with my partner

☐ sing songs

☐ learn about real things

☐ do experiments

☐ read and act out stories

☐ draw and write

2   Look at the 9 units in your Learner's Book.
Which unit was your favourite unit?

_____

Acknowledgements

The authors and publishers acknowledge the following sources of copyright material and are grateful for the permissions granted. While every effort has been made, it has not always been possible to identify the sources of all the material used, or to trace all copyright holders. If any omissions are brought to our notice, we will be happy to include the appropriate acknowledgements on reprinting.

Thanks to the following for permission to reproduce images:

Cover: Omar Aranda (Beehive Illustration); Mosutatsu/GI; Turnervisual/GI; Hdagli/GI; Vstock LLC/GI; Atw Photography/GI; undefined undefined/GI; ineskoleva/GI; Diane Labombarbe/GI; sodafish/GI

GI = Getty Images

The authors and publishers would like to thank the following for reviewing Stage 1: Jordan Olson, Judy Casiechetty, Nidhi Chopra

Development of this publication has made use of the Cambridge English Corpus (CEC). The CEC is a multi-billion word computer database of contemporary spoken and written English. It includes British English, American English and other varieties of English. It also includes the Cambridge Learner Corpus, developed in collaboration with Cambridge Assessment English. Cambridge University Press has built up the CEC to provide evidence about language use that helps to produce better language teaching materials.